Global Warming

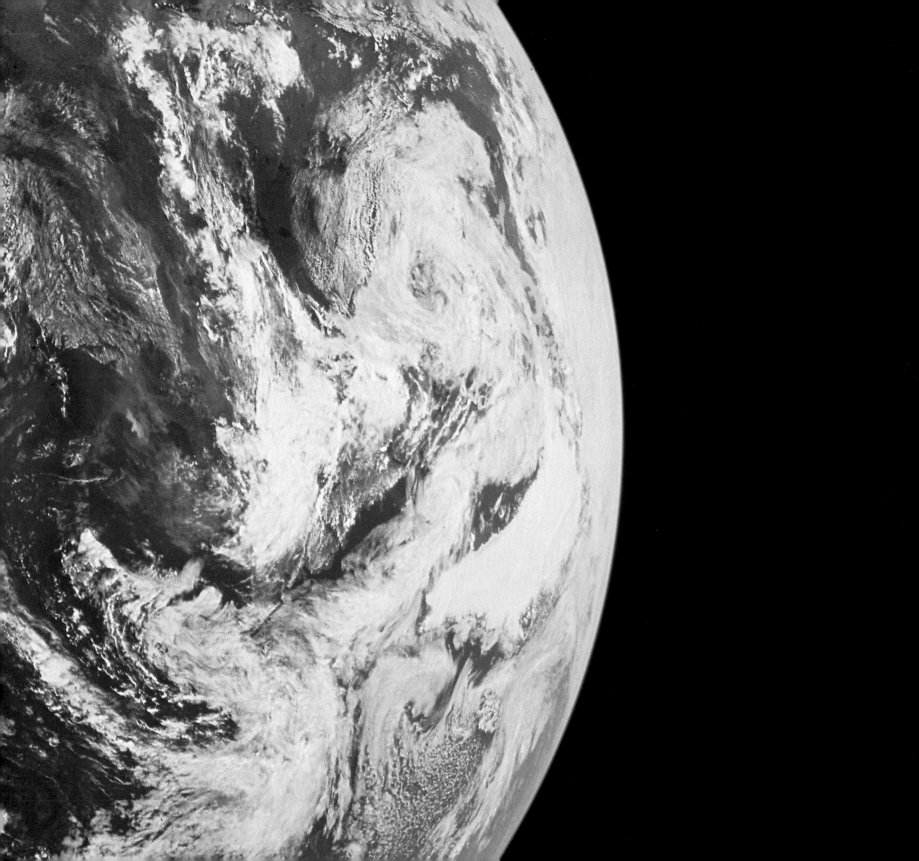

Laurence Pringle

Global Warming

Arcade Publishing | **New York** LITTLE, BROWN AND COMPANY

The author thanks Dr. George M. Woodwell, director of the Woods Hole Research Center, Massachusetts, for reading the manuscript of this book and helping to improve its accuracy.

First Edition

Library of Congress Catalog Card Number 89-82204
Library of Congress Cataloging-in-Publication Data is available.
ISBN 1-55970-012-2

Published in the United States by Arcade Publishing, Inc., New York, a Little, Brown company

Published simultaneously in Canada by Little, Brown & Company (Canada) Limited

PRINTED IN HONG KONG
SC

10 9 8 7 6 5 4 3

Photo Credits

Electric Power Research Institute, 40
International Stock Photography Ltd., © Ian Steele, 28 (top)
Chester C. Langway, Jr., State University of New York at
    Buffalo, 12
NASA, 1, 2, 18
Netherlands Board of Tourism, 32
Laurence Pringle, 11, 15 (both), 17, 21, 23 (both), 33, 36, 42
United States Geological Survey, 20
Visuals Unlimited, 26
    © Walt Anderson, 14 (left), 31, 39 (left)
    © John D. Cunningham, 27
    © Frank M. Hanna, 24
    © Steve McCutcheon, 8, 9, 22 (top), 38
    © Joe McDonald, 28 (bottom)
    © David Newman, 22 (bottom)
    © G. Prance, 39 (right)
    © Jeanette Thomas, 6
    © Tom Ulrich, 14 (right)
Scott Willis, *San Jose Mercury News*, 41
Ian Worpole, 29; Ian Worpole / Discover Publications (©
    1988, Discover Publications) 10, 30

Contents

Global Warming Has Begun

The earth is getting warmer. The changes are small, so far, but they are expected to grow and speed up. Within the next fifty to one hundred years, the earth may be hotter than it has been in the past million years.

As oceans warm and glaciers melt, land and cities along coasts may be flooded. Heat and drought may cause forests to die and food crops to fail. Global warming will affect weather everywhere, plants and animals everywhere, people everywhere.

Humans are warming the earth's atmosphere by burning fuels, cutting down forests, and by taking part in other activities that release certain heat-trapping gases into the air. Humans can solve the problem, too, but to find solutions people all over the world will need to cooperate more than they ever have before.

This book tells why the earth's climate is warming. It explores the effects that have begun and those that scientists forecast for the decades ahead. And it describes what people must do in order to prevent a worldwide disaster of their own making.

Climates Change

Weather changes from day to day, and may also change somewhat from year to year. The area where you live may have an occasional drought, or an unusually cold winter. Variations like these are part of overall climate—the weather that prevails in a particular area over the years.

You can often find different climates in places that are very close to one another. For example, the year-round climate on the north side of a tree or house is cooler than the south side, where more sunlight falls. The earth has a great range of climates, from the frigid polar regions to the hot tropics of the equator.

People expect weather to change but assume that climates are constant. However, climates have changed dramatically throughout the earth's history. Picture the conditions "just" 18,000 years ago—a short time in the life of a planet that is more than four billion years old:

The last Ice Age was at its peak. Sea level was more than one hundred feet lower and a broad land bridge existed between North America and Siberia. Glaciers that towered up to two miles high covered much of North America and northern Europe. The last of these vast ice sheets melted about seven thousand years ago, bringing the earth's oceans to their present levels.

Ice Ages are probably caused by regular changes in the earth's orbit around the sun and in its tilt toward the sun. These changes reduce the amount of solar energy reaching the earth, cooling its climate.

Ice Ages are inevitable, and scientists believe the next one will come—perhaps ten thousand years from now—despite human activities that are warming the earth. We cannot avoid a future Ice Age. We can, however, do something about troublesome changes in the earth's climate that we are bringing on ourselves.

Most glaciers and icebergs are now found near the earth's poles. In past Ice Ages, huge glaciers advanced far toward the equator.

Some solar energy is reflected into space from clouds and from ice and snow. Solar energy that strikes the earth's surface changes to heat (infra-red) energy. Some of this energy also escapes the earth's atmosphere. Other infra-red energy warms the earth. Human activities release gases that trap more heat in the atmosphere.

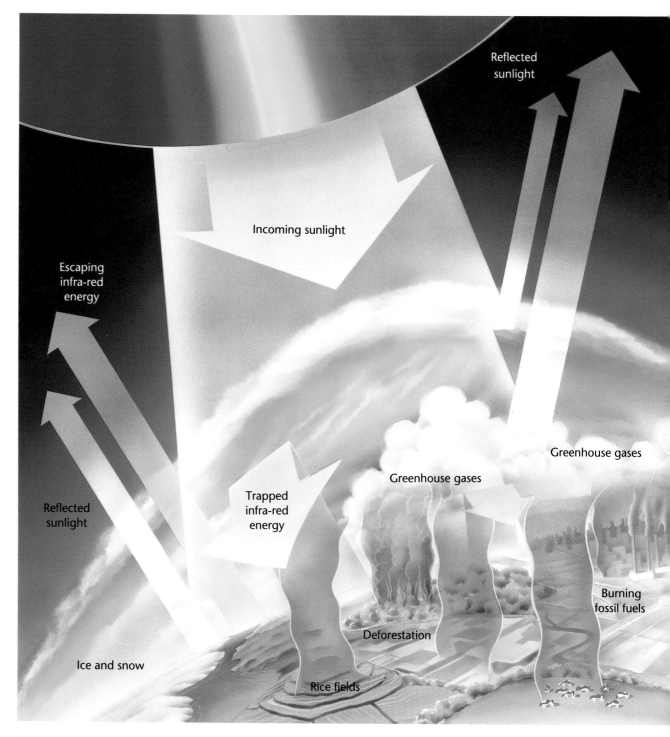

Reflected sunlight

Incoming sunlight

Escaping infra-red energy

Greenhouse gases

Greenhouse gases

Reflected sunlight

Trapped infra-red energy

Burning fossil fuels

Deforestation

Ice and snow

Rice fields

The Greenhouse Effect

The earth is covered by a thin blanket of gases called the atmosphere. Nitrogen and oxygen make up more than ninety-nine percent of the atmosphere. Nitrogen is about seventy-nine percent; oxygen about twenty percent by volume. Without oxygen there would be no life on our planet. It enables both plants and animals to "burn" food for energy. It also enables people to burn fuels for warmth, cooking, transportation, and manufacturing.

Compared to oxygen and nitrogen, there is only a trace of carbon dioxide in the earth's atmosphere—now just .035 percent of its dry volume. But this gas, along with water vapor, is also vital for life on earth.

When sunlight strikes the earth's surface, it is changed to heat (infra-red) energy. Some of this heat energy is absorbed by soils, plants, and water on the earth's surface. A lot of it is reflected back toward space. Not all of it is lost, however.

A greenhouse's roof of glass or plastic traps heat energy from the sun.

Molecules of carbon dioxide and other similar gases absorb this radiant heat and warm the atmosphere. The gases that absorb radiant heat include water vapor and methane but not abundant nitrogen and oxygen. Because these "trace" gases are present in such small quantities, a small change in their concentration has a large effect on the temperature of the earth.

Carbon dioxide, other trace gases, and water vapor in the atmosphere act somewhat like the windows of an automobile on a summer day. The

11

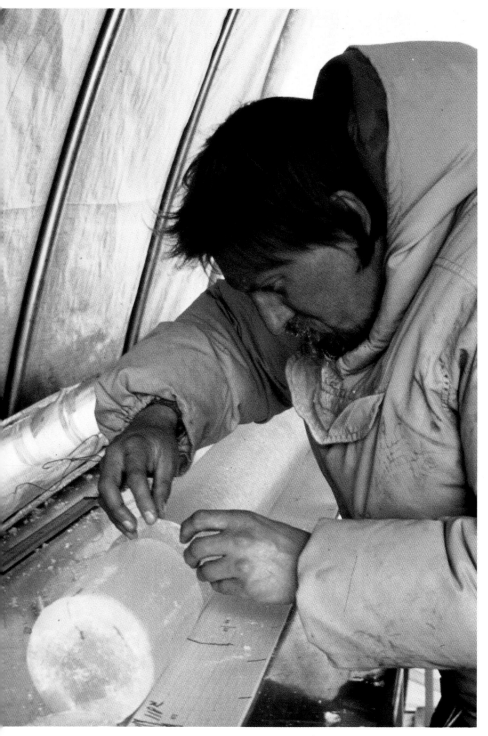

glass lets sunlight in but keeps heat from escaping. In the same way, glass or plastic in a greenhouse traps heat and protects plants from cold. This is called the greenhouse effect.

Like the earth, the planet Venus also has a greenhouse effect. Its atmosphere is so rich in carbon dioxide, however, that its surface temperature is about 860 degrees Fahrenheit. In contrast, icy Mars has a thin atmosphere with no water vapor and little carbon dioxide.

Both Mars and Venus are lifeless. People can be thankful for the small amounts of carbon dioxide and the water vapor in the earth's atmosphere. Without these gases, scientists estimate that the earth's surface temperature would be below freezing.

S The Carbon Cycle

Scientists learn about the earth's past atmosphere by studying glaciers in Greenland and Antarctica. As they drill through layer after layer of ice that once fell as snow, they find air bubbles from earlier times. These gas bubbles within glaciers are air samples of the past. From them we have learned that the amount of carbon dioxide in the earth's atmosphere has changed as temperatures and other conditions have changed over thousands of years.

Carbon dioxide enters the air during a

12

natural process called the carbon cycle. Carbon is a common element on earth. It is present in some kinds of rocks and in coral reefs. Vast amounts of carbon are also stored for a time in soils, in ocean waters, and in sediments at the bottom of the oceans.

When carbon is freed from rocks by erosion, it combines with other elements to form carbon compounds, including carbon dioxide. Green plants take carbon dioxide from the air. Within plants, carbon is converted to compounds that make up leaves, wood, and other plant parts, including seeds, fruits, and leaves that people eat. People, other animals, and plants give off some carbon dioxide as they "burn" these carbon compounds, and as they decay after death.

Every time you breathe you release some carbon dioxide. It may be taken up by a plant, the soil, the ocean, or some other part of the carbon cycle. For 160,000 years this natural cycle has kept the amount of carbon dioxide in the atmosphere at less than 300 parts per million.

Drilling more than a mile deep in Greenland glaciers, scientists have collected cores of ice formed a hundred thousand years ago. Studies of gas bubbles in the ice have revealed changes in the earth's atmosphere.

Adding Greenhouse Gases

The amount of carbon dioxide in the atmosphere began to increase in the nineteenth century, especially after the beginning of the Industrial Revolution. Carbon compounds are part of fossil fuels—coal, oil, and natural gas. When these fuels are burned, carbon combines with oxygen to form carbon dioxide. Human use of fossil fuels has quickly added large amounts of this gas to the atmosphere. In the 1980s, burning of fossil fuels released about 5.6 billion tons of carbon dioxide annually.

Cutting down forests also adds carbon dioxide. When wood decays, it releases its carbon slowly. When wood burns, most of its carbon escapes quickly in the form of carbon dioxide. Each year, many square miles of forest

are burned to clear land for farming, especially in the tropics. This deforestation releases at least a billion tons of carbon dioxide each year. Furthermore, it wipes out the trees that would normally remove some of the gas from the air and store carbon in the form of wood and other tissues.

As a result, carbon dioxide levels in the atmosphere are now twenty-five percent higher than they were in 1860. They reached 340 parts per million in 1987. These levels are already higher than at any time in human history. If people continue to burn fossil fuels and destroy forests, the concentration of carbon dioxide in the atmosphere may reach 600 parts per million midway through the next century. This alone could raise global temperatures higher than they have been at any time in the past 100,000 years.

People are also releasing several other heat-trapping gases into the

The burning of forests and especially of coal and other fossil fuels adds several billion tons of carbon dioxide to the atmosphere each year. Rice fields and decaying garbage release methane, another heat-trapping gas.

earth's atmosphere. These gases add to the greenhouse effect.

Methane gas is released during coal mining and the production of petroleum products. Natural gas *is* methane, so any leaks during the production, distribution, or use of natural gas add methane to the atmosphere. Methane is also produced when forests and grasslands burn, but mainly when once-living materials decay. It arises wherever decay occurs and little oxygen is present—from swamps and rice paddies, from garbage buried in landfills, and even from the guts of cows and termites.

The concentration of methane in the atmosphere has grown along with the human population. Worldwide, cattle are one of the greatest sources of methane. The earth's cattle population has doubled in the past forty years. There is now one cow or steer for every four people. Each one converts between three and ten percent of its food into methane.

During the 1980s, methane levels rose one percent each year. Methane is not nearly as abundant as carbon dioxide. In 1988 its concentration was 1.7 parts per million. However, methane is chemically twenty times more effective than carbon dioxide as a heat-trapping gas.

Human activities also add nitrous oxide, another heat-trapping gas, to the atmosphere. It is released wherever nitrogen-based fertilizers are spread on soils to increase food production.

Gases called chlorofluorocarbons, or CFCs, also cause the earth's climate to grow warmer. They are used as coolant gases in refrigerators and air conditioners, as insulation, and as propellant gases in spray cans. High in the earth's atmosphere, long-lasting CFCs destroy ozone, which shields the earth from harmful incoming ultraviolet rays. Also, a CFC molecule is ten

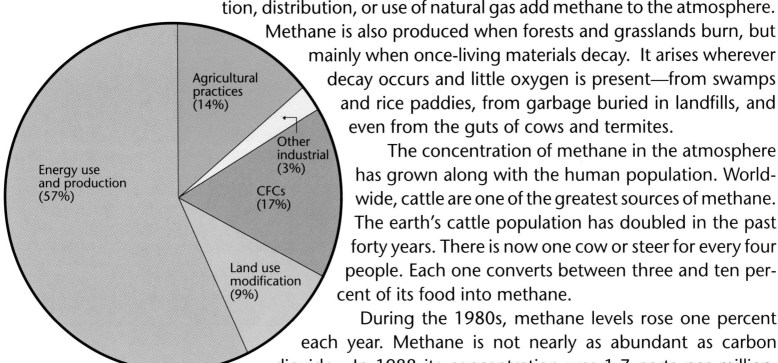

According to the Environmental Protection Agency, these were the human activities that added greenhouse gases to the atmosphere in the 1980s.

thousand times more effective than a molecule of carbon dioxide at absorbing heat.

Altogether, CFCs, methane, nitrous oxide, and a few other trace gases produced by human activities may be trapping as much heat in the atmosphere as carbon dioxide. Together with carbon dioxide, these gases are called greenhouse gases by scientists. Evidence shows that they are adding to the natural greenhouse of the earth's atmosphere and have already begun to warm the earth's climate.

Visible air pollution is only a small part of the global warming threat. Invisible greenhouse gases rise from countless sources.

A Warming Earth

Several years in the 1980s were among the warmest ever recorded on earth. But weather does change, so this hot spell alone does not prove that our planet's climate is changing. Evidence of change comes from study of temperature records from all over the world that stretch back to 1860. The records show that the average global temperature has increased about one degree Fahrenheit to fifty-nine degrees Fahrenheit (thirty-three degrees Celsius).

Some scientists have wondered whether the changes in temperature observed might simply be a result of the growth of cities near weather stations. Urban areas are "heat islands": pavement and rooftops absorb and store more heat than soils and plant leaves, so cities have warmer climates than rural areas. This factor was taken in account, however, and climatologists still found a worldwide increase in temperature. Also, ocean temperatures, measured far from cities, have been on the rise.

The earth's vast oceans have a powerful effect on climate, and for a time will slow global warming.

In the Southern Hemisphere, the warming is greatest over Australia, southern South Africa, the southern tip of South America, and the area of Antarctica near Australia. In the Northern Hemisphere, warming is strongest in Alaska, northwest and eastern Canada, most of the Soviet Union, and parts of southern Asia, north Africa, and southwest Europe. Climate has cooled in Great Britain and northern and eastern Europe. In the United States (excluding Alaska and Hawaii), scientists found no overall warming trend in weather records kept since the nineteenth century. Keep in mind, however, that the contiguous United States covers only 1.5 percent of the earth's surface. As warming continues, every place on earth will be affected.

Given the increase in greenhouse gases in the atmosphere, climatologists wonder why the earth's temperature did not rise higher in this century. The ocean may have delayed the warming by absorbing some of that increased heat. The effects of greenhouse gases may also have been offset by a temporary cooling trend. Between 1940 and 1970 the atmosphere actually cooled. The amount of radiation from the sun declined a bit, as it does from time to time. (Although energy from the sun has been called "the solar constant," scientists know that the sun's output of radiant energy varies by about one tenth of one percent over an eleven-year cycle.) Also, an unusual number of erupting volcanoes threw enough dust into the air to reduce the sunlight reaching the earth's surface, thereby cooling it.

The decade of the 1980s signaled an end to this cool period. It was the warmest decade on record, but only a taste of what may lie ahead.

Throughout history, dust from volcanic eruptions has caused temporary cooling of the earth's atmosphere.

20

Clouds usually shield about half of the earth's surface from direct sunlight. Their effect on overall climate is still not well understood.

Dirty Crystal Balls

No scientist claims to be able to predict changes in the earth's climate well into the next century. Scientists admit that there are many uncertainties in the methods they use, which some have called "dirty crystal balls."

Actually, they use mathematical models and powerful computers. The models are sets of equations that express the workings of the earth's atmosphere. However, we don't understand the atmosphere's full complexity, so some parts of the mathematical models may be inaccurate and some features of the atmosphere may not be included.

Oceans play a large role in the earth's weather patterns. The best computer models take the upper layers of oceans into account but not possible changes in the deep waters where so much carbon dioxide is stored.

Troublesome feedback factors include melting of snow on arctic tundra and warming of ocean waters. Both might cause further warming of the global climate.

Until 1989, most computer models of the atmosphere also failed to include the effects of clouds, which cover about half of the earth. Clouds reflect sunlight away from the earth. This tends to cool it. However, clouds are mostly water vapor, which helps trap heat in the atmosphere. Overall, most climatologists believe that the warming effect of clouds is slightly stronger than their cooling effect.

As greenhouse gases increase and warm the earth, clouds may change. Global warming could affect the types of clouds, their altitude, and their water content. Changes in clouds could then, in turn, affect global warming. An increase in high, wispy cirrus clouds would allow more solar energy to reach the surface. An increase in lower, thicker clouds would reflect more solar radiation than usual. Atmospheric scientists are trying to understand the effects of clouds on climate, and include them in their models of the atmosphere.

Clouds are an example of a feedback factor that may influence the rate of change in the world's climate. Scientists have identified several other feedback factors. Some may hasten global warming. Some may slow it. Here are a few of them:

• Most of the sunlight falling on snow and ice is reflected back toward space. As the climate warms, there will be less snow and ice. The sunlight will fall instead on darker soils and plants, which readily absorb sunlight. This will warm the earth further, causing even more snow and ice to melt.

• An increase in carbon dioxide stimulates plant growth in certain circumstances. In turn, the growing plants take in more carbon dioxide. However, there is a limit to how much of this gas plants can use.

• A warmer earth climate will speed the decay of dead plant material, resulting in the release of more carbon dioxide into the atmosphere. This will heat the earth's surface even more, further increasing the rate of decay and adding even more carbon dioxide to the atmosphere.

• Warm water absorbs less carbon dioxide than cold water. As the climate heats up, the oceans will take in less carbon dioxide. This will make the atmosphere and the oceans even warmer, and further reduce the ocean's capacity to absorb carbon dioxide. If the natural mixing of ocean waters lessens, the process of carbon dioxide sinking to the deep waters may be slowed.

Even the best models of the earth's climate do not include all of these and other feedbacks. Scientists say they do not know enough about most feedbacks to include them in their mathematical models.

Some people question whether the earth is growing warmer. They point to flaws in climatic models and to gaps in our understanding of the earth's atmosphere-ocean system. They warn about making forecasts based on the conditions of a few years or decades. In the early 1970s, for example, some climatologists looked at the 1940-1970 cooling trend and worried about a coming Ice Age.

Nevertheless, many climatologists believe that the evidence points to a warming climate. They expect the signs of climate change to become more clear in the 1990s. And their computer studies agree in general about changes and problems that rising temperatures may bring.

As temperatures rise, dead leaves decay more quickly, releasing greenhouse gases that may cause even greater warming.

A sea level rise of just a foot or two would cause great damage on coasts all over the world.

Rising Seas

In the frozen heart of the last Ice Age, 18,000 years ago, the temperature was only about nine degrees Fahrenheit colder than today. So a change of a few degrees can have dramatic effects. Today's most sophisticated climatic models estimate that global temperatures will rise between three and nine degrees Fahrenheit in the next century. This could occur as early as the year 2030. Here are the large-scale changes this warming might bring:

As water warms it expands, taking up more space. So warmer ocean water, with added meltwater from glaciers, will rise by twenty inches to five feet in the next fifty to one hundred years.

Just a one-foot rise in sea level can cause shorelines to recede a hundred feet, and in flat terrain, a thousand feet. If ocean waters rise several feet, whole beaches will wash away. Many homes, hotels, other buildings, and entire cities will be threatened. Salt water will pollute freshwater wells that millions of people use for drinking water. Coastal marshes, which are vital nurseries for fish and other ocean life, will be endangered. Along undeveloped coasts, marshes may survive because they can move inland with the rising waters. In many places, however, seawalls and other human structures will prevent this process and the marshes will be destroyed.

Low-lying land areas are especially vulnerable to rising seas. Some islands in the Caribbean, the Marshall Islands in the Pacific, and the Maldive Islands west of India could disappear entirely. In the United States, ocean water may cover the Florida Keys and large parts of southern Florida and Louisiana.

Flat river delta areas are most vulnerable to rising seas. Vast amounts of fertile land will be lost at the deltas of the Ganges River in Bangladesh, the Indus in Pakistan, the Yangtze in China, the Nile in Egypt, and the Magdalena in Colombia. Egypt could lose fifteen percent of its best farmland, which is also home for fourteen percent of its people. Bangladesh already suffers when ocean storms flood its vast delta region. Rising seas would surge much farther inland and could eventually cover more than ten percent of the entire country.

Changing Weather Patterns

The second major effect of global warming will be changes in weather—temperatures, amounts and patterns of precipitation, and frequency and intensity of storms. Temperatures will rise more swiftly in the Northern Hemisphere because it holds less ocean water to absorb heat than in the Southern Hemisphere.

In both hemispheres, scientists predict, the farther from the equator, the greater the rise in temperature. And there will be greater warming in winters than in summers. So if global temperatures rose 3.6 to 5.4 degrees Fahrenheit, the winter temperatures in Minneapolis, Minnesota, would rise between 7.2 to 10.8 degrees Fahrenheit. Winter temperatures would rise by an even greater amount in the Arctic and Antarctic.

Besides melting snow and ice, rising temperatures will dry soils, rivers, and lakes through the process of evaporation. Increased evaporation puts more water vapor in the atmosphere. This will produce more worldwide rain and snow, but weather patterns may shift, bringing droughts to some regions, increased rain to others.

Oceanic currents are generated in part by contrasts in temperature between masses of water. Global warming may cause currents to slow down or shift direction. This could affect fish populations and the climates of coastal areas. The Gulf Stream now warms Great Britain. Winters there would be much colder if this current slowed. Overall warming of oceanic waters will also give rise to more frequent and more powerful hurricanes.

Food production and water supplies could drop in such key areas as the central plains of the United States and Canada. Farmers there now export grains to countries that cannot produce enough food for their citizens.

Hurricanes will become stronger and more frequent as ocean temperatures rise. On land, rainfall patterns are likely to change in unpredictable ways.

Global warming may destroy forests and wildlife over large areas. As past Ice Ages came and went, forest plants and animals had thousands of years to adapt to changing conditions. When the climate warmed, forests and wildlife species gradually moved northward. This natural process requires centuries, not a few decades.

Many species may become extinct as their habitats disappear. There is no way to protect national parks or other nature reserves from global warming. The natural world of the year 2050 and beyond may be only a sad remnant of today's rich variety of plants and wild animals. Small, mobile organisms would be less vulnerable to rapid change, and some might thrive in a warming climate. Unfortunately, they include disease-carrying mosquitoes, parasites, and pests of crops and livestock.

Although scientists agree on the broad effects of global warming, their computer forecasts differ on regional changes. Some areas may benefit from global warming. India, for example, might receive increased rainfall that would aid agriculture. Farmers in Canada and the Soviet Union might also benefit from a warmer climate.

There is no way to know in advance the winners and losers of global warming. No nation can *plan* on gaining. With the prospect of food and water shortages, increased tension between rich and poor nations over scarce resources, and stressful changes people may face as they try to cope with the effects of global warming, it seems likely that every person will suffer in one way or another. Furthermore, unless something is done, greenhouse gases will continue to increase. Temperatures could soar higher and higher.

What changes might unchecked global warming bring? Scientists have identified one disastrous possibility: the freeing of the West Antarctica ice

Global warming could reduce supplies of food and drinking water in regions already suffering from shortages. It could also melt sea ice where polar bears, seals, and other animals live part of each year.

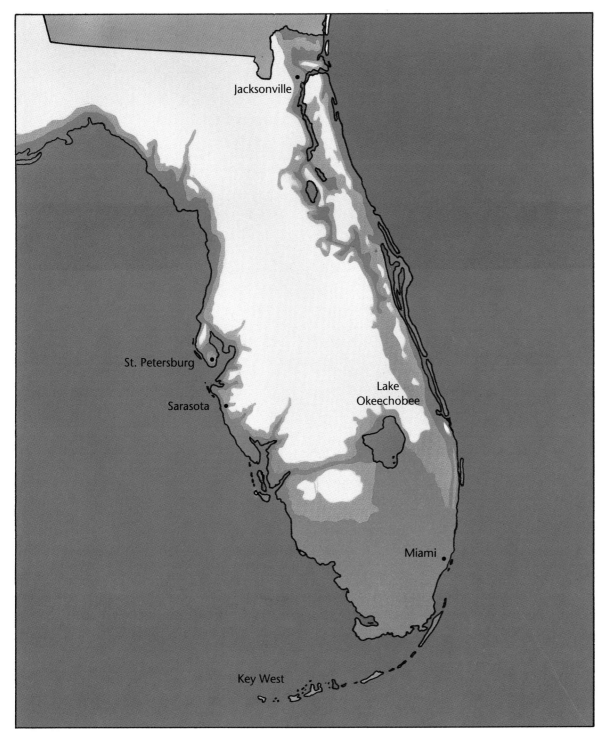

Jacksonville

St. Petersburg

Sarasota

Lake
Okeechobee

Miami

Key West

The present sea level around Florida and its Keys is shown in blue. Ocean waters could cover the area shown in dark green if the West Antarctica ice sheet floated free. Unchecked global warming could raise sea levels 25 feet above normal, covering the area shown in light green.

sheet. This vast chunk of ice, 1.2 million cubic miles in size, rests on bedrock. If Antarctica warmed enough so that this ice sheet broke free and floated, the addition of its volume to the ocean would quickly raise sea level an estimated sixteen to nineteen feet. A gigantic surge of water would invade coasts all over the world. Many port cities would be underwater. In California, San Francisco Bay would reach more than thirty miles inland, flooding the Sacramento Valley.

According to one computer model, a doubling of carbon dioxide in the atmosphere would cause these changes (explained in color key) in the earth's soil moisture in summer, when food crops are grown.

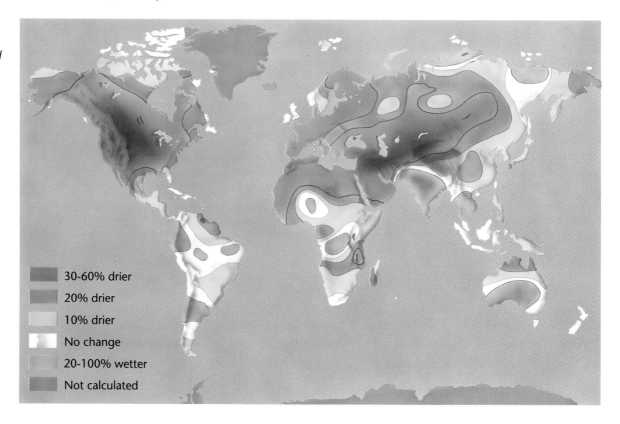

30-60% drier
20% drier
10% drier
No change
20-100% wetter
Not calculated

Adapting to a Warmer World

Two kinds of action are called for. One is to take steps to prepare for the effects of warming that already seem inevitable. Agricultural scientists must develop varieties of wheat and other crops that can thrive in a longer but drier growing season. Ways must be found to use irrigation water more effectively. Conservation will also be vital for drinking-water supplies.

Governments that control building and other development along coasts must begin to plan for rising sea levels. In the United States, billions

In regions where rainfall decreases, growth of irrigated crops may have to be curtailed.

31

of dollars have been spent to replace sand eroded from beaches, and to help owners of beachfront homes rebuild after storm damage. Efforts like these would be foolish in the face of rising seas. The states of Maine and North Carolina now prohibit permanent buildings on threatened beaches.

Retreat from the sea seems wise, but impractical in the case of cities and such costly structures as nuclear power plants. Dikes and levees can protect them—at great cost. About half of the Netherlands is below sea level, and the Dutch have spent billions of dollars to build and maintain 250 miles of dikes and 120 miles of dunes. Imagine the cost of defending much longer coastlines against steadily rising seas.

Massive and costly dikes can protect some coastal areas, as they do in the Netherlands.

Everyday life in industrialized nations produces most of the carbon dioxide from fossil fuels and other greenhouse gases emitted in the world.

Reducing Greenhouse Gases

People living in cold climates may welcome a little warming. But most atmospheric scientists agree that people must act soon in order to limit the warming to "a little."

One of the easiest steps is to stop use of CFC gases. They are doubly harmful, trapping heat in the atmosphere and also destroying the earth's ozone layer. This allows more cancer-causing ultraviolet light to reach the surface. The ultraviolet light itself also changes the heat balance of the

33

atmosphere. As it penetrates closer to the earth's surface, it causes lower layers of the atmosphere to grow warmer.

Canada and the United States banned the use of CFC gases in aerosol cans in the 1970s. In 1989, delegates from eighty nations met in Helsinki, Finland, and agreed that all use of CFCs must end by the turn of the century. Manufacturers of refrigerators and other products in which CFCs are used are rapidly developing substitutes.

Banning these greenhouse gases is simple, compared with the challenge of reducing other greenhouse gases, especially carbon dioxide. It is a byproduct of countless human activities, including transportation, manufacturing, growing food, and heating, cooling, and lighting homes and businesses.

Scientists estimate that a fifty-percent cut in emissions of carbon dioxide is needed to halt its increase in the atmosphere. Since industrialized nations produce most greenhouse gases, they must take the first and biggest steps. Delegates to the 1988 International Conference on the Changing Atmosphere, held in Toronto, Canada, called for industrialized nations to reduce carbon dioxide emissions by twenty percent by the year 2005.

To achieve this, nations must begin to switch from coal and oil to other fuels. Coal-burning electric plants in the United States produce 7.5 percent of all carbon dioxide going into the entire atmosphere. Burning natural gas produces half as much carbon dioxide as coal. Wood and other plant material (including paper separated from household waste) produces less carbon dioxide than coal but more than natural gas.

No carbon dioxide at all comes from some other energy sources, including nuclear power. However, many people are concerned about nuclear power's cost and safety, including the disposal of nuclear wastes. Clean, safe

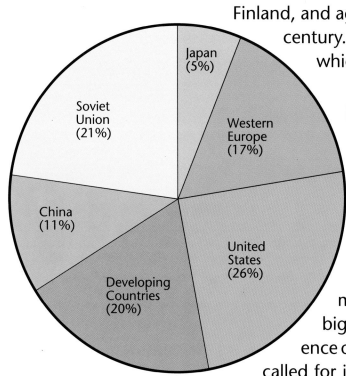

In the 1980s, industrialized nations produced 80 percent of the earth's emissions of carbon dioxide.

sources of electricity include water, wind, and solar power. Several small solar energy plants already generate electricity in California. The cost of making electricity from sun energy is dropping, and energy experts say that many utilities will build solar electric plants early in the next century.

Great cuts in carbon dioxide emissions can be achieved by burning less fuel for heating and transportation. This is especially true in the United States, which wastes much more energy than other industrialized nations. Its automobiles use more fuel, and produce more carbon dioxide, than those of Japan, West Germany, and many other nations.

Cars in the United States get an average of 18.3 miles from a gallon of gasoline. Replacing these vehicles with cars that get double the mileage per gallon would cut the country's emissions of carbon dioxide by one-eighth. Fuel used to heat buildings could also be cut sharply by such steps as adding insulation and replacing windows that easily lose heat. These steps could dramatically cut carbon dioxide emissions in the United States. Such nations as Japan and Sweden face a greater challenge in reducing carbon dioxide. They already use energy quite efficiently.

Carbon Dioxide Emissions from Fossil Fuels		
Source	Carbon Dioxide (million tons)	Carbon Dioxide Per Person (tons)
USA	4480	18.37
USSR	3711	13.07
W. Europe	2899	7.61
China	2031	1.90
Japan	908	7.43
India	549	.70
Canada	388	14.93
World	19438	3.88

According to the Oak Ridge National Laboratory, in 1987 the United States emitted the equivalent of more than 18 tons of carbon dioxide for every citizen.

Engineers and scientists may develop substitutes for gasoline fuel. Hydrogen gas can be used as fuel for automobiles, although its separation from water requires electricity. In the near future, however, the greatest challenge is to cut emissions of carbon dioxide in the world's industrialized nations. A "carbon use tax" would be one way to encourage this. People, manufacturers, and electric utilities would pay added fees for using fossil fuels. Coal would be taxed the most because it contains the most carbon.

A Reforesting the Earth

A third of the earth's forests have been cut down in the past 10,000 years, since people began practicing agriculture. In recent years the pace of deforestation has quickened. In the 1980s about 4,400 square miles were cleared annually. This deforestation adds great amounts of carbon dioxide to the atmosphere.

Trees store carbon for long periods. Any plan for reducing global warming must include reforestation.

Scientists urge that forest-clearing be slowed, and also advocate a major reforestation effort. All plants take in carbon dioxide and store some carbon, but trees, because of their size and long lives, play a major role in the earth's carbon cycle. Reforesting an area the size of Alaska would remove about a billion tons of carbon from the atmosphere. In the tropics, at least two million square miles of cleared land could be reforested.

Planting trees seems wise for other reasons. In cities they have a cooling effect. This reduces the need for air conditioning, and, in turn, the need for electricity generated by burning fossil fuels. Tree-planting programs can slow the pace of global warming, buying time for the vital but difficult steps needed to burn less fossil fuel.

T Conflict or Cooperation?

here are plenty of good ideas for reducing greenhouse gases. And we already have the devices and materials needed to use fuels more efficiently. The question remains: Will people all over the world cooperate and take the steps needed to halt global warming?

Industrialized nations account for about thirty percent of the earth's population, but produce about seventy-five percent of greenhouse gases. Clearly, they must "go first" in reducing emission of these gases. Their actions can show the way.

Scientists and environmental groups in the United States have urged Brazil and other Latin American nations to halt deforestation. Meanwhile, the U.S. Forest Service allowed increased cutting of mature rain forest in the Pacific Northwest and Alaska. This was hardly setting a good example.

Even if industrialized nations lead the way, will less developed Third World countries follow? Most of them are burdened by debt and growing populations. They aim to industrialize, as other nations have, by burning fossil fuels. Consider China, home of one-sixth of the earth's population. It plans to spur development by doubling its use of coal as fuel in the next fifteen years. And consider the rapid destruction of tropical rain forests. Most of the trees are not replaced with the goal of sustaining forests and having future harvests. Most are cut and burned by landless people desperate for a place to grow food.

Coal being loaded onto a barge in the Yangste. China has planned on coal to fuel its industrial development.

38

Global warming cannot be stopped unless China and other developing nations are persuaded to bypass fossil fuels as the key to industrialization. The United States and other developed countries must go beyond setting a good example. They must help Third World countries develop in ways that halt deforestation and reduce emissions of greenhouse gases.

One step would be to upgrade systems of distributing electric power. In India, for example, this would halve the losses from the existing power

system, so that India wouldn't need to generate as much electricity. Also, many Third World nations lie in the tropics, where solar energy is abundant all year. They stand to gain the most from development of low-cost solar electric power. This technology is being developed in the earth's rich nations. By speeding its development, they can help Third World nations onto a solar energy path that turns away from fossil fuels.

People in many tropical nations destroy forests in order to grow food. Unless this practice changes, there is little hope of halting global warming.

The Greatest Challenge

There is broad agreement among atmospheric scientists that the threat of global warming is real and that we must act quickly to minimize its damage. Nevertheless, some scientists, politicians, and industry leaders urge a "wait and see" policy. They advocate more study but argue against costly steps to reduce greenhouse gases.

Some people believe that global warming might be avoided by painting the roofs of all buildings white and by spreading white plastic chips on the ocean's surface. This would reflect more sunlight into space. So would spreading dust in the atmosphere. Others suggest fertilizing ocean waters to stimulate growth of tiny plants that take carbon dioxide from the air. Still others advocate development of huge satellites that would orbit the earth and cast shadows on its surface.

Most scientists question the wisdom of these and other schemes aimed at making large-scale changes in the earth's atmosphere-ocean system. Tinkering with something we don't understand very well could make things worse.

Uncertainty about some details of global warming should not be used as an excuse for inaction. Besides, the steps needed to reduce greenhouse gases make good sense for other reasons. By burning less fossil fuel, people save money and reduce air pollution. They also gain by using fuels more efficiently. Halting deforestation will reduce erosion and the loss of many unique plants and animals that might someday prove to be invaluable to people.

It is time to act against global warming. An international "Law of the Atmosphere" may be necessary, with all nations agreeing to cut emissions

Solar energy may offer tropical countries an alternative to burning fuels that produce greenhouse gases (left).

of greenhouse gases. The cost of delay could be disastrously high for all people on earth. Sometime in the next century their numbers will double. The need for food and energy will grow. Meeting these needs while reducing greenhouse gases is the greatest challenge ever faced by the human species, calling for extraordinary cooperation among nations. Can humankind rise to this challenge?

Glossary

atmosphere   the whole mass of gases that surrounds the earth. The earth's atmosphere reaches 400 miles above the surface, but eighty percent of its air is concentrated in the troposphere, which extends seven miles upward. Although nitrogen and oxygen make up ninety-nine percent of the earth's atmosphere, other atmospheric gases are vital for the survival of life on earth.

carbon dioxide   a colorless, odorless gas that forms when carbon atoms combine with oxygen atoms—for example, during the process of burning or decay. Carbon dioxide is a small but vital part of the atmosphere. It is a key ingredient in photosynthesis, the process in which green plants make the food upon which all animals depend. Its heat-trapping characteristic helps make life on earth possible.

chlorofluorocarbons (CFCs)   gases used as coolants in refrigerators and air conditioners, as foaming agents for insulation and food packaging, and as cleaning agents in certain industries. Their use as propellant gases in aerosol cans has been phased out in many nations. CFCs are long-lasting compounds that absorb infra-red energy more effectively than carbon dioxide. In the upper atmosphere, chlorine from CFCs destroys ozone that protects life on earth from harmful ultraviolet radiation.

climate   the weather conditions that prevail in a particular area. Climates of rather small areas (for example, of one side of a valley or a tree) are called microclimates.

climatologists   scientists who study climates. Others who are involved in learning about global warming include computer programmers and scientists who study oceans, glaciers, weather, and the atmosphere.

evaporation   the process by which a liquid is changed to a gas, usually water into water vapor.

feedback   a change caused by a process that, in turn, may influence that process. Some changes caused by global warming may hasten the process (positive feedback); some may slow it (negative feedback).

fossil fuels   fuels containing carbon that are believed to have formed from living materials millions of years ago. Coal, natural gas, and petroleum are fossil fuels.

greenhouse effect   a warming effect that occurs in the earth's atmosphere as carbon dioxide and other gases absorb heat energy or reflect it toward the earth's surface. The greenhouse effect makes the earth habitable. On Venus, however, a "runaway" greenhouse effect creates conditions too hot for life.

infra-red   invisible heat radiation that is emitted by the sun and by virtually every warm substance or object—rocks, water, buildings, hot coals, and living things, including humans.

methane   a colorless, odorless, flammable gas that is the major ingredient of the fuel called natural gas. Methane is produced wherever decay occurs and little or no oxygen is present.

molecule   the smallest possible amount of a compound that still has the characteristics of that substance. A molecule of carbon dioxide consists of two atoms of oxygen and one of carbon.

nitrogen   in gaseous form, nitrogen takes up four-fifths of the volume of the earth's atmosphere. Nitrogen is also an element in such substances as proteins, fertilizers, and ammonia.

nitrous oxide   a gas emitted from nitrogen-based fertilizers. Nitrous oxide is another human-produced gas that traps heat in the earth's atmosphere.

ozone a form of oxygen present in the earth's atmosphere in small amounts. A layer of ozone, between fourteen and nineteen miles above sea level, makes life possible by shielding the earth's surface from most ultraviolet rays. Ozone can be produced by people and is used to purify water and as a bleaching agent. As an air pollutant, ozone damages materials and living tissues, and causes headaches and burning eyes.

tundra treeless habitat of the Arctic. Beneath its covering of mosses, lichens, and stunted shrubs lies permafrost—subsoil that is frozen year-round.

weather conditions of the atmosphere at a particular time and place, including temperature, precipitation, air pressure, and wind speed and direction.

ultraviolet invisible radiation from the sun that has shorter wavelengths than visible violet light. Ultraviolet light includes tanning rays but also more powerful wavelengths that cause sunburn and skin cancer. Most of these damaging rays are blocked from reaching the earth's surface by a layer of ozone gas in the stratosphere.

Index

This book was designed by Marc Cheshire on an Apple Macintosh SE computer using PageMaker 3.01 software. An Apple LaserWriter II NT was used to output page proofs for proofreading. The final pages were output as one-piece repro on a Linotron 300 typesetter at 1,270 dots-per-inch resolutition.